D0393112

Taking care of your

RABBIT

A Young Pet Owner's Guide
by Helen Piers

Consulting Editor: Matthew M. Vriends, Ph.D.

BARRON'S

First edition for the United States and Canada
published 1992 by Barron's Educational Series, Inc.
Text copyright © Helen Piers 1992
Illustrations copyright © Helen Piers 1992

First published in Great Britain in 1992 by
Frances Lincoln Limited, Apollo Works
5 Charlton Kings Road, London NW5 2SB

All rights reserved.
No part of this book may be reproduced in any form,
by photostat, microfilm, xerography, or any other
means, or incorporated into any information retrieval
system, electronic or mechanical, without the written
permission of the copyright owner.

All inquiries should be addressed to:
Barron's Educational Series, Inc.
250 Wireless Boulevard
Hauppauge, NY 11788

Library of Congress Catalog Card No. 91-26710

International Standard Book No. 0-8120-4697-8

Library of Congress Cataloging-in-Publication Data
Piers, Helen.
    Taking care of your rabbit/Helen Piers: consulting editor,
Matthew M. Vriends.
        p.   cm. — (A Young pet owner's guide)
    Includes index.
    Summary: Offers advice on selecting, feeding, housing, and
maintaining the health of a pet rabbit.
ISBN 0–8120–4697–8
    1. Rabbits—Juvenile literature. [1. Rabbits as pets.]
I. Vriends, Matthew M., 1937–   .   II.Title.   III. Series: Piers,
Helen. Young pet owner's guide.
SF453.2.P53   1992
636'.9322—dc20   91-26710
                                                          CIP
                                                           AC

Printed and bound in Hong Kong

3 4 5   9 8 7 6 5 4 3 2

Contents

Rabbits as pets 4

Which breed? 6

One, two, or more? 7

Things you will need 8

The hutch 10

Getting the hutch ready 12

Buying rabbits 14

Feeding 1 16

Feeding 2 18

Handling rabbits 20

Cleaning and grooming 22

Exercise 24

Health 26

Illnesses 28

Unexpected babies 30

More about rabbits 31

Index 32

Rabbits as pets

Rabbits make very lovable pets. They are gentle, good-tempered animals, and if handled kindly become very tame.

Rabbits have been bred as pets for hundreds of years, yet pet rabbits still have the same nature and instincts as wild rabbits. They tend to be timid and easily frightened, even though they are no longer in danger from predators as they would be in the wild. That is why they have to be handled gently.

Pet rabbits need to be let out regularly to hop about, explore, and feel the ground under their feet, just as a wild rabbit does when it comes out of its burrow to forage for food. And they need company, because it is natural for rabbits to live in family groups. A rabbit kept on its own will be lonely unless it gets a lot of human companionship.

If it is handled gently and often enough, a rabbit soon learns to trust people.

If you decide to keep rabbits, apart from the initial cost of a hutch and perhaps an outdoor run, they are not expensive or difficult to care for, but there are a few things you should think about to make sure you will be able to look after them well.

Do you have a yard?

If not, would friends let your rabbits exercise in their yard sometimes, either free or in a run?

Do you have time to look after rabbits?

You will need to feed them twice a day, let them out to pet every day, and clean their hutch regularly.

Is there a grown-up who will help you?

You may need help with the cost of housing and feeding, or if your rabbits are ill.

Do you have friends to feed and keep an eye on the rabbits when you go on vacation?

A rabbit has large, mobile ears, and its eyes are positioned on either side of its head so it can hear and see all around without moving. In the wild, rabbits have many predators, and must always be on their guard.

Wild rabbits get exercise outside their burrows foraging for food. A pet rabbit's food is brought to it, but it will get very bored, and even bad-tempered, unless it is allowed out of its hutch often enough, to run about and explore.

Which breed?

There are a number of different breeds of rabbits to choose from, and different colors of coat are found in all breeds.

The small (called *dwarf*), and medium-sized breeds make the best pets. The bigger rabbits are more difficult to handle.

Do not choose a longhaired breed (*Angora*) unless you really have time to brush and comb it every day.

Crossbreeds (rabbits that have a mother of one breed and a father of another) also make very good pets.

Photographed on this page are three of the more suitable breeds, but of course there are different color varieties within each breed.

A Netherland dwarf
This is a very small rabbit, and can be recognized by its short ears. Adult weight: 2 to 3 pounds.

A dwarf lop
The ears of this rabbit bend over and hang down on either side of its head. Adult weight: 4 to 5 pounds.

Two Dutch rabbits
These are very placid and gentle. They can have differently colored coats, but they usually have a white "blaze" down the center of the face. Adult weight: 5 to 6 pounds.

One, two, or more?

One rabbit

A rabbit can be kept on its own, but only if it has a lot of human companionship. *Bucks* (males) and *does* (females) make equally good single pets.

A lonely rabbit can be given a guinea pig as a companion when grazing out-of-doors, but because many vegetables that guinea pigs need are not good for rabbits, they should be given the evening feeding apart, and also housed separately at night.

Two rabbits or more

Two bucks should never be kept in the same hutch. When grown-up, they will probably fight. But *two does* (or three, if the hutch is big enough) will live together happily. They will be company for one another and keep each other warm in winter. It is best to buy sisters from the same litter. Strangers may be put together while under ten weeks old, but must be watched at first to make sure they get along.

A buck and a doe can be kept together, but of course, they will mate and have babies. A doe can have eight or even more babies in one litter, and seven litters a year. That is a lot of young rabbits to find homes for! The mother and babies need special care, and the father must be moved to another hutch, in case he harms the babies.

Breeding rabbits is not recommended unless there is a grown-up to help.

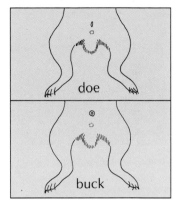

Telling a buck from a doe
Get a grown-up to help you do this. Hold the rabbit on its back, so that a vent, or small opening near the anus, can be seen, then *very gently* press on either side of this. If it is a buck, the penis will protrude as a small rounded tip. If a doe, only a small slit will show.

Things you will need

Checklist

- hutch
- outdoor run
- wood shavings
- oat straw
- food dishes
- drip-feed water bottle
- food:
  rabbit pellets *or*
  cereal mix
  fresh vegetables
  hay
- small block or branch
  of hardwood
- cleaning materials
- extras:
  litter box
  hay rack
  carrying box
  grooming brush

A hutch

Oat straw for bedding

Wood shavings (or wood chips) for the hutch floor. Make sure these have not been treated with chemicals.

A movable outdoor run

A block or branch of hardwood for the rabbits to gnaw prevents their teeth from growing too long.

Heavy earthenware food dishes are best — they cannot get knocked over.

A drip-feed water bottle is better than a bowl, as it keeps the water clean.

Food (see checklist)

(see checklist)

Never

On the hutch floor

Never use sawdust instead of wood shavings — it is too fine. It gets into the rabbits' eyes, and is bad for their breathing.

Wood for gnawing

Never give softwood — it splinters too easily. *Never* give laburnum, azalea, holly, purple thorn-apple, or evergreen wood — they are poisonous. Wood from fruit trees is best. *Never* put anything made of thin plastic in the hutch — the rabbits may chew it, and swallow bits that they cannot digest.

A litter box

Cleaning materials

A hay rack

A grooming brush

The hutch

Pet stores sell rabbit hutches, or you may be able to buy one secondhand, borrow one, or build your own.

Important points about the hutch
Is it big enough?
Is it safe from other animals?
Is it easy to keep clean?
Is it weatherproof?

The best place to keep the hutch
Rabbits need air and light, but dampness, really bitter cold, and extreme heat are dangerous for them. Rabbits like company and are happiest if the hutch is situated where there are people around, or within hearing distance.

Out-of-doors
Rabbits are hardy enough to live outside, but you must find a place out of the wind, sheltered as much as possible from rain, and shaded from hot midday sun. In freezing weather, give extra bedding and cover the hutch with plenty of old rugs or blankets.

Indoors
You can keep the hutch indoors if there is plenty of fresh air and light, but *not* beside a radiator, or in a draft, or by a window that gets midday sun.

One or two dwarf or medium-sized rabbits need a hutch at least 35 × 17½ × 17½ inches, but 59 × 23½ × 23½ inches would be better. Rabbits must be able to sit up easily on their hindquarters.

A hutch raised off the ground will be dry and safe from other animals, including wild rabbits which might spread myxomatosis.

The roof must be sloping, covered with roofing felt, and overhang the sides to keep off the rain. In heavy rain, a sheet of polythene hung down in front of the hutch will keep the rain from coming inside.

In very hot weather, some types of roof can be propped open to let in air. But *not* if any cats are around!

Never

Never put the hutch in a greenhouse or under a glass roof — it would get dangerously hot.
Never put it in a garage that is in use — gas fumes are poisonous.

The hutch can be kept on a balcony as long as it is not exposed to cold winds or hot midday sun. Other good places could be against a sheltering wall, in a porch, or in a light and airy shed.

The hutch should have a light daytime area with a wire mesh door, and a smaller, dark sleeping area with a solid wood door. Both doors must fasten securely.

Getting the hutch ready

A homemade hutch costs less than a ready-made one, and is not hard to build, but make sure it is weatherproof.

If possible, get the hutch ready and comfortable before you bring your rabbits home.

First, scrub it out with a teaspoon of mild disinfectant in soapy water. *Rinse and dry it well.*

Then put several sheets of newspaper and a layer of wood shavings — about ¾ inch deep — over the floor, and pile plenty of straw in the sleeping area.

Put the food dishes and wood for gnawing in the light daytime area. Attach the water bottle to the wire mesh door.

A layer of newspaper under the wood shavings makes cleaning out the hutch easier.

A litter box

Rabbits usually choose to wet and leave their droppings in one corner of the hutch. If you put a litter box there, and empty it daily, the hutch will stay much cleaner.

A hay rack

A hay rack is not essential, but it prevents the hay from getting trampled and dirty before it is eaten. If you cannot find one in the pet store, you can make one out of wire — but make sure there are no sharp ends that could scratch a rabbit.

A carrying box

You can buy a carrying box in which to bring the rabbits home, or use a securely-closed cardboard box. If your trip will take more than four hours, you will need a wooden box. Make sure your box has enough air holes, and put newspaper, some straw, and a little food in the bottom.

This hay rack has been made out of an old wire letter tray. It is hung on cup hooks, screwed into the wall of the hutch.

This litter box is made of Teflon. Enamel or earthenware could be used, but ordinary tin will rust. Never use thin plastic, which the rabbits will nibble.

Buying rabbits

Don't be in a hurry to choose your rabbit. Take time to watch which ones come to you without fear. A rabbit's temperament is as important as its looks.

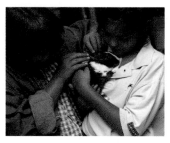

If you like a particular rabbit, ask if you can hold it to see if you feel comfortable with it. At the same time, check that it is healthy. This little rabbit is fine and seems used to being handled.

Most pet stores sell rabbits, or you may have a friend who is looking for homes for young ones, or you may be able to buy one straight from the breeder.

There are some important things to find out about the rabbits you choose.

How old are they?
Between seven and ten weeks old is best.

What will they weigh when full-grown?
Under 6 pounds, they will be easier to handle.

Are they bucks or does?
Don't forget: two adult bucks cannot be kept in the same hutch.

Are they healthy rabbits?

A healthy rabbit should be bright-eyed and alert.

Its coat should be smooth, glossy, clean, and without any bare patches.

Its eyes and nose should not be runny.

Its ears should be clean inside, without any black specks or crusty material.

What food have they been used to?

You should give the same for the first week. After that, if you prefer, you can introduce other foods, but only gradually. A sudden change of diet can give rabbits stomach upsets.

Taking them home

Make your journey home as short as possible. If you go by car or train, rest the box on your knee so the rabbits do not get jolted. Talk to them quietly to give them confidence. Take care that they do not get too hot.

Remember

● How old are the rabbits?
● What will they weigh when full-grown?
● Are they bucks or does?
● Are they healthy?
● What food are they used to?

When you get home, put your rabbits gently into their hutch. Give them food and water, and leave them alone and quiet to recover from the journey, and get used to their new home.

It is kinder to wait until the next day before you play with them or show them to friends.

Feeding 1

Rabbits eat mostly cereals (such as wheat, oats, and barley), vegetables, and hay.

Cereals

You can buy special cereal mix (sometimes in the form of pellets) from pet stores. This contains all the nutrients a rabbit needs. If ever you run out, you can mix crushed or rolled oats or crumbled *wholemeal* bread with a little warm milk or water as an emergency supply.

rabbit pellets

rabbit mix

carrots

parsnips

spinach

turnips

Some vegetables for your rabbits

Vegetables

Rabbits need both root and green vegetables, but *green* vegetables must be given with care. *Do not give green vegetables to rabbits under twelve weeks*, and only a little to dwarf breeds of any age. The exception is cauliflower leaves and stalk — the part that usually is thrown away.

Rabbits like lettuce, but it is really *not* good for them.

Remember

- Feed at the same time every day.
- Remove uneaten food from the day before.
- Wash vegetables and fruit well.
- Give raw, fresh vegetables — not cooked or frozen.
- A mixture of vegetables is better than a lot of one kind.
- Make sure clean, dry hay and fresh water are available at all times.
- Introduce any new kind of food gradually.

cauliflower stalk and leaves

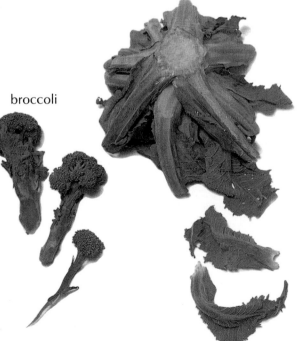

broccoli

parsley

string beans

peas (and pods)

(More about feeding on the next page.)

Feeding 2

Hay

It is important that rabbits always have hay available. It is a valuable source of fiber.

Wild plants

Do not gather wild plants for your rabbits unless you are sure you can recognize the right ones — *many wild plants are poisonous.* Some that are good for them are clover, dandelion leaves, grasses, nettles, shepherd's purse, sow-thistle, mallow, and yarrow.

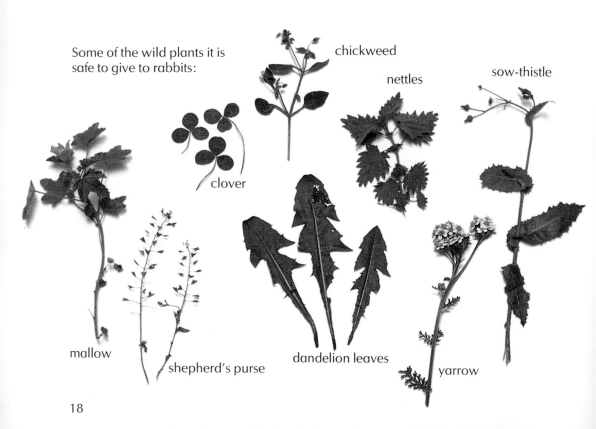

Some of the wild plants it is safe to give to rabbits:

chickweed

nettles

sow-thistle

clover

mallow

shepherd's purse

dandelion leaves

yarrow

Food needed by one rabbit:

In the morning
   One cup of pellets or rabbit mix.

In the evening
   Two handfuls of mixed fresh vegetables.

Give hay and fresh water at both meals.

   If food is left uneaten, give less next time. If it all is eaten, try giving more. Rabbits do not overeat.

Never

Never give green vegetables to rabbits under twelve weeks old. *Never* gather wild plants from beside a busy road, because of pollution, and *never* from a lawn sprayed with pesticides.
Never give grass cuttings or raw potato peelings.
In spring, *never* let your rabbit eat too much white clover or wet grass, that can make it very ill.

You can give a little fruit to your rabbits, but only as an occasional treat. Some suitable fruits are apples, blackberries, pears, raspberries, and strawberries.

19

Handling rabbits

To pick up a rabbit, grasp it firmly, but not tightly, by the scruff of the neck with one hand, and slide the other under its hindquarters. As you lift it, keep your arm close to your body. Never lift a rabbit by the scruff without supporting its weight with the other hand.

If you find it difficult to hold your rabbit by the scruff, slide one hand under it from the side, close behind its front legs, so that it is resting on your palm. Grasp it gently with your thumb on one side, fingers on the other. Your other hand must support its hindquarters.

To hold a rabbit, let it sit firmly on one hand and rest along your arm. Keep your arm close to your body, so that the rabbit is leaning against you. Your other hand is free to support it, or restrain it if it gets restless.

Always put your rabbit into its hutch backwards, then if for some reason it gets frightened and kicks out with its back feet, it will not bruise you, or make you drop it.

Don't forget rabbits are easily frightened, so although you should handle them firmly — they must not feel that you might drop them — at the same time, be gentle and quiet. Try not to make jerky movements, shout, or talk loudly.

If you are nervous about handling your rabbits, practice picking them up and holding them while kneeling on the ground until you are confident. Then if you do drop them, they will not get hurt.

It is important to handle your rabbits for a short time every day if possible. Talk to them and call them by name. They will get to know their names, and the sound of your voice.

Never

Never pick up a rabbit by its ears.
Never stroke its fur the wrong way.
Never grab it, hold it too tight, or squeeze it.
Never overtire it by handling it for too long.

Remember

- Handle your rabbits for a short time, but often and regularly.
- Handle them firmly but gently, and they will learn to trust you.
- Always hold them close to your body, so they feel secure.
- Try not to be nervous when you handle your rabbits — that will make *them* nervous too.
- Always pick up and hold them in the same way, so they get used to it and know what to expect.

Cleaning and grooming

It is very important for your rabbits' health to keep the hutch clean and dry. It need not be an unpleasant job, if done often enough.

Once a day
Clear away leftover food, and wash food dishes.
If using a litter box, empty it, and refill with fresh wood shavings.

Every other day
Clear out daytime area, throw dirty wood shavings on the compost heap or in a garbage can, and put down fresh.

Once a week
Clear out sleeping area as well as daytime area, and give fresh bedding straw.

Once a month
Clear out, then wash whole hutch with a teaspoon of disinfectant in the water. *Rinse and dry well*, in the sun if possible.

If you have put newspaper under the wood shavings, it is easy to lift out and empty them into a bucket or garbage bag. A paint scraper is useful for getting into dirty corners.

When a rabbit grooms itself, you will see it pays special attention to its ears — licking its paws, wiping them over the ears, then licking them again. It has been discovered that it is not only cleaning its ears but also conveying small amounts of natural oil from the ears to its mouth. This oil is rich in vitamin D, which a rabbit needs for healthy bones.

Rabbits keep clean by grooming themselves and each other, but it is good to give them a gentle brushing regularly. They enjoy it, it makes them more friendly, and it gets rid of loose hairs when they are molting.

Never bathe your rabbit.

A *longhaired* rabbit will need more grooming. Tangles should be teased out gently with a metal comb before brushing, and badly matted hair may have to be cut away with blunt-ended scissors.

Be very gentle when you groom your rabbit. Never brush its fur the wrong way, and do not poke its eyes.

Exercise

You can let your rabbits run free in the yard, provided it is well fenced or walled in, and not so big that if they hide, you cannot find them. Also, if very tame, they may not be on guard against cats or dogs. Be careful!

A safe way to give rabbits exercise is to buy or build them a portable run.

Better still, the hutch can be kept in an enclosure, fenced in with wire netting, so the rabbits can come out and run about when they feel like it. If they dig a few holes, nobody will mind, for this is their own bit of the yard. The fence needs to be sunk 1 foot or more into the ground, so they cannot burrow under it, and

A rabbit may be hard to catch when you want it to go back into the hutch. Try not to frighten it by pouncing and grabbing. Quietly back it into a corner. It will know when it can't escape and let you pick it up. This sounds easy. It isn't. Be patient.

This kind of run is called an *ark*. It is roofed at one end to give shelter from sun and rain, and the rest covered with wire mesh. It can be moved easily from one part of the yard to another.

be 7 feet high to keep other animals out. The rabbits must be shut in the hutch at night.

Some rabbits can be allowed to exercise and play in the house, because you can train them to wet in a litter box like a cat.

If your rabbit makes a puddle on the carpet, it is no good punishing it. It won't understand. Just wash the wet place, put the litter box close by, and show it to your rabbit. It should soon begin to use it to wet in all the time. Rabbit droppings are dry and can be swept up.

See that your rabbit does not chew the furniture, or, more dangerous, any electric wiring.

Remember

● Make sure your rabbits cannot escape by squeezing through a narrow gap or burrowing under a fence.
● Check that they have shelter from both sun and rain, and are safe from other animals.
● Always put fresh water within reach.
● Do not let them out in very cold or wet weather.
● Shut them in the hutch at night.
● Indoors, watch out for electric and telephone wiring.

If you let your rabbit run about indoors, you can use a deep cat litter box for it to wet in. If the litter box is made of thin plastic, see that your rabbit does not nibble it.

Health

Remember

You will help your rabbits stay healthy if you:
- Feed them correctly.
- Give them hay and fresh water at all times.
- Never give a new kind of food without trying a small bit first to see if it agrees with them.
- Provide hardwood for gnawing.
- Keep the hutch clean and *dry*.
- Never let your rabbits get wet, too hot, or too cold, and make sure they have enough exercise and company.

Rabbits are not good at fighting illness, so if your rabbit is sick, *do not put off taking it to your veterinarian.*

How do you know if a rabbit is ill?

It may not eat. It may sit hunched up, or lie stretched out on its side, its eyes dull. It will not twitch its nose, or take notice when you talk to it. It may drink more than usual. It may have diarrhea.

What to do if a rabbit is ill

There is some advice on the following page, but the veterinarian will know best. You can always telephone the veterinarian and explain things. The veterinarian will tell you whether or not you should take your rabbit in to be looked at. Meanwhile, make sure it has plenty of fresh water, and is warm enough.

If you are at all worried that your rabbit may be sick, take it to the veterinarian, who will know if there is anything seriously wrong.

It is worth taking your rabbits for a checkup about once a year. At the same time, the veterinarian will look at their claws. Rabbits' claws sometimes grow too long and cause them pain. Do not try clipping them yourself.

Sometimes a sick rabbit gets well sooner if moved from the place where it first got ill. In any case, if you have more than one rabbit in the hutch, you should move the sick one to a comfortable box elsewhere. It is less likely then to pass on any illness to the others.

If one of your rabbits dies

Through no fault of yours, your rabbit may get ill, and the veterinarian may be unable to save it. If your rabbit does die, and you have nowhere to bury it, the veterinarian will look after this for you.

It will be sad when your rabbits die, even if quite naturally of old age. The important thing is to know you have given them the very best life you could. Don't forget, pet rabbits cannot look after themselves as they would if they were living wild. Your rabbits depend on you for everything they need.

Rabbits' teeth go on growing throughout their lives, and if allowed to get too long, prevent them from eating. That is why rabbits must always have hardwood to gnaw on and wear their teeth down. The veterinarian will trim your rabbits' teeth if they need it. It will not hurt.

Illnesses

These are some of the more common illnesses rabbits may suffer from, with a little advice about what to do.

Symptoms	Possible cause and what to do
The rabbit does not eat, and makes almost no droppings	It may have *constipation*. Remove dry food. Give only hay, water, carrot and apple. A teaspoon of medicinal liquid paraffin may help.
The droppings are runny and sour smelling	The rabbit has *diarrhea*. Remove all food except hay. **Give plenty of fresh water**, and a few well-washed dandelion leaves. If no better in a few hours, **take it to the veterinarian**, as prolonged diarrhea can be fatal.
The rabbit's stomach is swollen and hard, and it is short of breath	This may be *bloat* (bad wind). The rabbit may have eaten too much green food. This can happen when a rabbit is let out in the yard in early spring and eats too much young white clover and wet grass. Bloat is a very serious illness so **get your rabbit to the veterinarian as soon as you can**. Meanwhile give half a teaspoon of liquid paraffin, and remove all food including hay.
Bare patches in the fur	This might be caused by *mites*. The veterinarian will advise treatment.
Overgrown claws or teeth	See page 27.

Runny nose and sneezing	The rabbit has a *cold*. Keep it warm. Sprinkle a few drops of oil of eucalyptus on the bedding. If no better in two days, **take to the veterinarian**.
The rabbit lies at full length, panting rapidly	It has *heat exhaustion*. Put it in the shade at once. Give it water at room temperature. Hold a cool, damp cloth against its head and then its legs. In very hot weather, it is advisable to hose down the hutch to keep the rabbits cool.
The rabbit scratches behind its ears, and shakes its head	If there is dark brown, crusty matter deep inside its ears, this is *ear mites* (or *ear canker*). The vet will give you ointment or powder to clear them up.

Fleas

If your rabbits have fleas, sprays and powders for kittens can be used. But, of course, do not use a flea collar on your rabbit.

Cuts and wounds

Add a drop of mild antiseptic to warm water (boiled and allowed to cool), and bathe the wound gently. If it gets red and inflamed, **take your rabbit to the veterinarian**.

Electric shocks

If your rabbit has bitten through an electric wire, and is lying unconscious, or semiconscious, **call in your veterinarian at once**. Meanwhile, cover with a blanket and keep very warm.

Coprophagy or reingestion

You may see your rabbits seeming to eat their own droppings. This is quite natural. Rabbits have to digest their food twice, and what your rabbit is really doing is eating half-digested food.

Unexpected babies

Breeding rabbits is not recommended unless you are sure you can find homes for the young ones, but it might happen that your doe rabbit was pregnant when you bought her, and you find she is going to have babies you did not plan for. This will show only about a week before the babies are due, when she will be noticeably fatter. (A doe is pregnant for 28 days.)

If you think one of your rabbits is pregnant, you must house her separately, and make sure her hutch is clean, dry, and sheltered from cold in winter, and from hot sun in summer. Give her the same food, but more, plenty of water, and some soft hay for her nest. She will pull out some of her own fur to line the nest.

When the baby rabbits (kittens) are born *do not* touch the nest to look at them for two days, or the mother may be frightened, and attack them — her instinctive way of protecting them.

On the third day, you will need to find out if they are all right. Coax the mother away with food, then rub your hands in her dirty litter, so they smell right to her. Try not to disturb the nest too much. You will find the kittens are without fur and quite helpless. Some may not be alive. Remove these, and then cover the others up carefully.

You will find more detailed advice in the books listed on page 31, and your veterinarian will advise you if you have any problems.

At about three weeks, the babies will begin to come out of the nest and explore the hutch. A few days later, you should begin to handle them very gently for a few minutes each day; then they will always be very tame.

More about rabbits

Rabbits cannot tell you what they feel or want, but when you have had yours a little while you will find out how they behave when they are hungry, and when they want to be let out to run about or would rather be quiet.

As you get to know your rabbits, they will sense that you understand them and begin to trust you and enjoy your company. Some rabbits are more timid than others, but there are rabbits that enjoy human company so much that they will even jump up onto somebody's lap of their own accord.

Useful information

A doe is pregnant for	28 days
Kittens can leave their mother at	6–8 weeks
Females can breed at	5 months
Males can breed at	9 months
Rabbits are full grown at	15–18 months
Life expectancy	4 to 6 years or longer

Some rabbits are quite happy to be taken for a walk on a lead, and will wet outside. A cat harness is suitable for fastening the lead.
Never use a collar.

Further reading

Dwarf Rabbits
Monika Wegler
Barron's, Hauppauge, New York, 1986

Hop to It
Samantha Hunter
Barron's, Hauppauge, New York, 1991

The New Rabbit Handbook
Lucia Vriends-Parent
Barron's, Hauppauge, New York, 1989

Rabbits
Monika Wegler
Barron's, Hauppauge, New York, 1990

Index

Babies, 7, 30, 31
Bloat, 28
Breeding, 7, 30
Breeds, 6
Buck, 7, 14

Carrying box, 8, 13
Catching a rabbit, 24
Cereals, 16
Claws, 27, 28
Cleaning materials, 8, 9, 22
Colds, 29
Companionship, 4, 7, 10
Constipation, 28
Coprophagy, 29
Cuts, 29

Death, 27
Diarrhea, 26, 28
Doe, 7, 14, 30
Droppings, 13, 25, 28, 29

Ears, 5, 15, 23, 29
Electric shock, 29
Enclosure, 24
Exercise, 24–25

Feeding, 5, 15, 16–19
Fleas, 29
Food dishes, 8, 9
Fruit, 19

Grooming, 23
Guinea pig, 7

Handling, 15, 20–21
Hay, 8, 9, 13, 18, 19, 30
Hay rack, 8, 9, 13
Health, 15, 26–29
Heat exhaustion, 29
Hutch, 5, 8, 10, 11
    cleaning, 22

Illnesses, 28–29

Length of life, 31
Litter box, 8, 9, 13, 22, 25

Myxomatosis, 10

Nest, 30
Newspaper, 12, 22

Pellets, 8, 9, 16
Plastic, 9, 13
Pregnancy, length of, 30–31

Rabbit mix, 8, 9, 16, 19
Run, 8, 24

Straw for bedding, 8, 12, 22

Teeth, 27, 28

Vegetables, 8, 16, 17, 19
Veterinarian, 26–29, 30

Water bottle, 8, 9, 12
Wild plants, as food, 18, 19
Wood, for gnawing, 8, 9, 12, 27
Wounds, 29